HEAVEN

first steps

Heaven

What's it like?
How do we get there?

Created by
STEPHEN ELKINS

Illustrated by
KIRSTEEN HARRIS-JONES

TYNDALE KIDS

Tyndale House Publishers, Inc.
CAROL STREAM, ILLINOIS

Visit Tyndale's website for kids at www.tyndale.com/kids.

TYNDALE is a registered trademark of Tyndale House Publishers, Inc. The Tyndale Kids logo is a trademark of Tyndale House Publishers, Inc.

Heaven: What's It Like? How Do We Get There?

Copyright © 2014 by Stephen Elkins. All rights reserved.

Created by Stephen Elkins

Illustrated by Kirsteen Harris-Jones

Designed by Ron Kaufmann

Edited by Brittany Buczynski

Watercolor texture copyright © ilolab/Shutterstock. All rights reserved.

For manufacturing information regarding this product, please call 1-800-323-9400.

Library of Congress Cataloging-in-Publication Data

Elkins, Stephen.

  Heaven : what's it like? how do we get there? / created by Stephen Elkins ; illustrated by Kirsteen Harris-Jones.

     pages cm. -- (First steps series)

  ISBN 978-1-4143-7931-9 (hc)

  1. Heaven--Christianity--Juvenile literature. 2. Christian life--Juvenile literature. I. Jones, Kirsteen H., illustrator. II. Title.

  BT849.E55 2014

  236'.24--dc23

                2013030866

Printed in China

20   19   18   17   16   15   14

7   6   5   4   3   2   1

TABLE OF CONTENTS

Letter to Parents vii

What Is Heaven Like?

Heaven Is Real 2

Heaven Is Exciting 4

Heaven Is Big 6

Heaven Is Perfect 8

Heaven Is Beautiful 10

Heaven Is Safe 12

Heaven Is Forever 14

In Heaven We'll Sing 16

In Heaven We'll Rest 18

In Heaven We'll Receive Rewards 20

In Heaven We'll Praise Jesus 22

We'll See Angels in Heaven 24

We'll See Bible Heroes in Heaven 26

We'll See People from All Nations in Heaven 28

We'll See People in Heaven Who Lived Long Ago 30

We'll See Jesus in Heaven 32

Heaven Is Never Dark 34

Heaven Is Never Sad 36

Heaven Is Where God Lives 38

Heaven Is Where I Will Live 40

How Do We Get There?

Open God's Special Book 44

Discover Our Special God 46

Know God's Powerful Name 48

Believe That God Can Do Anything 50

Trust That God Knows Everything 52

God Made a Perfect Creation 54

God Made the First Man 56

Adam Made a Bad Choice 58

Sin Came In 60

Man Is Separated from God 62

God's Special Plan 64

Jesus Is Born 66

Jesus Lived a Perfect Life 68

Jesus Would Pay the Price 70

Jesus Gave His Perfect Life to You and Me 72

God Made Jesus Alive Again 74

Jesus Is Our Only Way to Heaven 76

Big Questions 78

Heaven's Prayer 80

Another House in Heaven 82

How Do We Live Like Jesus until Then?

We Live Like Jesus 86

We Love One Another 88

We Serve One Another 90

We Are Patient with One Another 92

We Care for One Another 94

We Are Kind to One Another 96

We Help One Another 98

We Fellowship and Play with One Another 100

We Speak the Truth to One Another 102

We Show Kindness and Mercy to One Another 104

We Are Faithful to One Another 106

We Show Hospitality to One Another 108

We Are Courteous to One Another 110

We Respect One Another 112

We Pray for One Another 114

We Comfort One Another 116

We Build Others Up 118

We Are Peacemakers 120

We Have Self-Control 122

We Are Joyful 124

Glossary of Bible Words 127

LETTER TO PARENTS

Hello, my name is Stephen Elkins. I am the author of this book: HEAVEN! I wrote this book to help children better understand some basic biblical facts about heaven. There are three parts, each built around a key question.

The first part is a beginner's course exploring the question *"What is heaven like?"* In the second part, we address the question *"How do we get there?"* which focuses on Jesus Christ and how He made a way for us to enter heaven. Finally, in the third part, we answer the question *"How do we live like Jesus until then?"* with many practical examples.

By reading this book together, you and your child will gain a confidence that heaven is a *real* place and a very *exciting* place! It will encourage you both to live in light of the fact that the Kingdom of Heaven is within you. I hope you will enjoy reading and discovering more about the wonderful place we call heaven!

BLESSINGS!
Stephen Elkins

NOTE: Words that appear LIKE THIS
are explained in the glossary at the back.

What Is Heaven Like?

HEAVEN IS REAL

God created everything in heaven and earth. He made the things we can see and the things we can't see.

COLOSSIANS 1:16

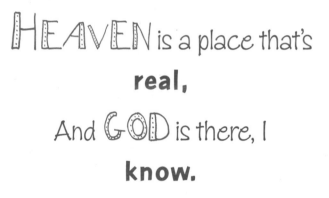

HEAVEN is a place that's **real,**

And GOD is there, I **know.**

This I believe with all my **heart.**

The Bible tells me **so!**

HEAVEN IS EXCITING

Yes, leap for joy! For a great reward awaits you in heaven.

LUKE 6:23

. . .

Heaven is an exciting
place,
An adventure land of
fun!

We meet new friends
every day
Who love Jesus,
every one!

HEAVEN IS BIG

He found out that the city was as wide as it was long and it was as high as it was wide. It was as long as a man could walk in fifty days.

REVELATION 21:16 (NLV)

• • •

Heaven is a great big

space,

So high and long on every

side.

Taller than a mountain

PEAK

And a million elephants

wide!

HEAVEN IS PERFECT

Be perfect, just as your Father in heaven is perfect.

MATTHEW 5:48 (NIrv)

Heaven is a perfect

place

So wonderful to

see.

Perfect like the

LAMB OF GOD,

Who died for you and

me!

HEAVEN IS BEAUTIFUL

The twelve gates were made of pearls. . . .
And the main street was pure gold.

REVELATION 21:21

• • •

The light of God is heaven's

light.

Its gates are precious

PEARLS.

The streets are paved with purest

gold

For special boys and

girls!

HEAVEN IS SAFE

Make sure your treasure is safe in heaven, where thieves
cannot steal it and moths cannot destroy it.

LUKE 12:33 (CEV)

In heaven we're safe

forever.

With peace that does

ASTOUND us.

For God is there to keep us

safe

His love is all

around us.

HEAVEN IS FOREVER

I will live in the house of the LORD forever.

PSALM 23:6

• • •

On earth, time passes

quickly.

All things soon fade

away.

So I can't wait for

heaven,

Where there's always one more

day!

IN HEAVEN WE'LL SING

All creatures in heaven . . . were singing.
I heard them say, "May praise and honor for ever and ever be
given to the One who sits on the throne."

REVELATION 5:13 (NIrV)

• • •

In heaven we'll hear songs of
PRAISE,

And with one voice we'll
sing:

"All glory to the Lamb of
God,

Our SAVIOR, King of
kings!"

IN HEAVEN WE'LL REST

I heard a voice from heaven saying,
". . . They will rest from their hard work."

REVELATION 14:13

Heaven is a place of

rest

Where we will live

together.

We'll run and play with our dear

friends.

We'll laugh and love

FOREVER.

IN HEAVEN WE'LL RECEIVE REWARDS

Be very glad! For a great reward awaits you in heaven.

MATTHEW 5:12

• • •

God has made a

PROMISE

To all who love the

Lord.

When we get to

heaven,

We'll get a great

REWARD!

IN HEAVEN WE'LL PRAISE JESUS

Rejoice with him, you heavens. And let all of God's angels worship him.

DEUTERONOMY 32:43

There's lots of love in **heaven,**
The kind that has no **end.**

There all CREATION **praises**
Jesus, our heavenly **friend.**

WE'LL SEE ANGELS IN HEAVEN

I looked and heard the voice of millions and millions of angels.

REVELATION 5:11 (NIrV)

Heaven is full of

ANGELS,

More than a million or

two.

Each one serving God with

joy.

Each one has a job to

do!

WE'LL SEE BIBLE HEROES IN HEAVEN

Abel . . . Enoch . . . Noah . . . Abraham . . . Sarah . . .
were [all] looking forward to a better home in heaven.

HEBREWS 11:4-16 (CEV)

• • •

In heaven we'll meet

HEROES

Who walked by FAITH each

day.

You can be a hero

too.

Just trust God and

obey!

WE'LL SEE PEOPLE FROM ALL NATIONS IN HEAVEN

I saw a vast crowd . . . from every nation and tribe and people and language, standing in front of the throne.

REVELATION 7:9

In heaven, we will meet the

SAINTS

From every TRIBE and NATION.

In every LANGUAGE they will

sing

To thank God for

salvation!

WE'LL SEE PEOPLE IN HEAVEN WHO LIVED LONG AGO

[Jesus said,] "I am not praying just for these followers.
I am also praying for everyone else who will have faith."

JOHN 17:20 (CEV)

• • •

Yes, we'll see Jesus in

heaven,

With David and Paul sing

praises!

For all who loved the Lord are

there

From all across the

ages!

WE'LL SEE JESUS IN HEAVEN

Because I am righteous, I will see you. When I awake,
I will see you face to face.

PSALM 17:15

• • •

Of all the joys that heaven

holds,

The greatest that will

please us

Will be to see our Savior's

face.

His PRECIOUS name is
JESUS!

HEAVEN IS NEVER DARK

There will be no more night.
REVELATION 22:5 (NIV)

· · ·

In heaven there will be no

night,

Just one forever

day.

No bedtime prayers are needed

there.

Dark nights are gone

away!

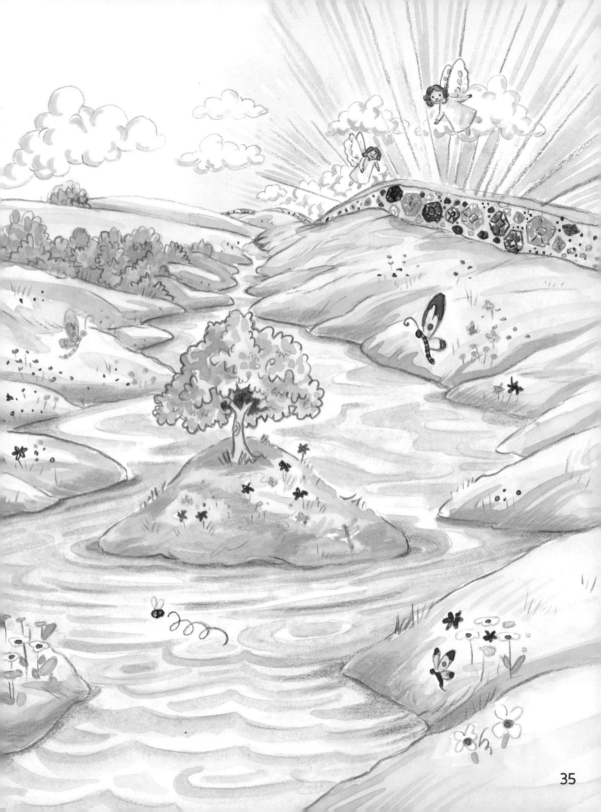

HEAVEN IS NEVER SAD

He will wipe every tear from their eyes, and there will be no more death or sorrow or crying or pain.

REVELATION 21:4

Heaven is a

happy place

With no more pain or

tears.

God will wipe them all

away

And comfort all our

fears.

HEAVEN IS WHERE GOD LIVES

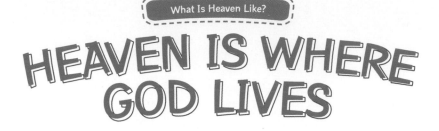

[Solomon prayed,] "Listen to us from heaven.
It's the place where you live."

1 KINGS 8:30 (NIrV)

Our loving FATHER has a

home

Somewhere far beyond the

stars.

He lives in heaven up

above,

Yet He lives within my

HEART!

HEAVEN IS WHERE I WILL LIVE

I will be there to greet you personally and welcome you home.

JOHN 14:3 (VOICE)

• • •

When Jesus comes to greet

me

And my name I hear Him

call,

Then my first words in

heaven

Will be "Thank You,

Lord of all!"

How Do We Get There?

OPEN GOD'S SPECIAL BOOK

All Scripture is inspired by God.

2 TIMOTHY 3:16

The story of God in

heaven

Is a story of His great

love!

It's found only in the

BIBLE,

A special book from God

above!

DISCOVER OUR SPECIAL GOD

For the LORD Most High is awesome.
He is the great King of all the earth.

PSALM 47:2

There's only one God and

Father.

His wonders each day we all

see.

Perfect in power and

WISDOM.

Forever His KINGDOM shall

be.

KNOW GOD'S POWERFUL NAME

The LORD is a warrior; Yahweh is his name!

EXODUS 15:3

Our God is great and **mighty!**

Creation does PROCLAIM

His power and His **glory.**

Lord YAHWEH is His **name!**

BELIEVE THAT GOD CAN DO ANYTHING

---•---

Is anything too hard for the LORD?

GENESIS 18:14

• • •

My God can do

anything.

So strong and powerful is

He!

His words can make a

forest

Or tiny birds up in a

tree.

TRUST THAT GOD KNOWS EVERYTHING

Your Father knows what you need before you ask him.

MATTHEW 6:8 (NIV)

There's nothing hidden from God's

sight,

On earth or under the

sea.

Before we even ask for

help,

He knows just what we

need.

GOD MADE A PERFECT CREATION

In the beginning God created the heavens and the earth.

GENESIS 1:1

• • •

God had a big

IDEA,

One only He could

do.

He'd make a sun, a moon, and

stars

So perfect and so

new!

GOD MADE THE FIRST MAN

Then the LORD God formed the man from the dust. . . .
He breathed the breath of life into the man's nostrils,
and the man became a living person.

GENESIS 2:7

Oh, such a perfect world God

made,

All CRAFTED by His loving

hand.

He made each cuddly

animal,

He made Adam, the very first

man!

ostrich

ostrich

horse

giraffe

llama

hippopotamus

lion

elephant

ADAM MADE A BAD CHOICE

Adam disobeyed God and caused many others to be sinners.

ROMANS 5:19 (CEV)

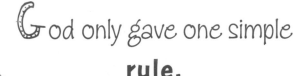

God only gave one simple **rule.**

One simple rule was **given:**

"Don't eat this fruit, or you will **die."**

But Adam didn't **listen!**

SIN CAME IN

Everyone has sinned; we all fall short of God's glorious standard.

ROMANS 3:23

• • •

SIN came in the heart of

man.

What is this "sin" we

do?

Sin is doing what WE

want,

Not what God tells us

to!

MAN IS SEPARATED FROM GOD

Your sins have SEPARATED you from your God. They have caused him to turn his face away from you. So he won't listen to you.

ISAIAH 59:2 (NIrV)

• • •

Oh how awful! Oh how

sad!

Why did you

DISOBEY?

God can never look on

sin.

He has to turn

away!

GOD'S SPECIAL PLAN

God loved the world so much that he gave his one and only Son.
Anyone who believes in him will not die but will have ETERNAL life.

JOHN 3:16 (NIrV)

• • •

The problem was a
big one!
Oh, what would poor Adam do
now?

Jesus would come from
heaven.
He'd solve the sin problem, but
how?

JESUS IS BORN

You . . . will name him Jesus—"God saves"—because
he will save his people from their sins.

MATTHEW 1:21 (THE MESSAGE)

As the angels sang "GLORY to
God,"
Baby Jesus slept in the
hay.

The Savior had come down from
heaven
To take all our sins far
away!

66

JESUS LIVED A PERFECT LIFE

Jesus understands every weakness of ours, because
he was tempted in every way that we are. But he did not sin!

HEBREWS 4:15 (CEV)

• • •

Remember ol' Adam? He
disobeyed!
But Jesus filled God with
DELIGHT!

Not once did He ever say something
wrong
Or do something that wasn't
right!

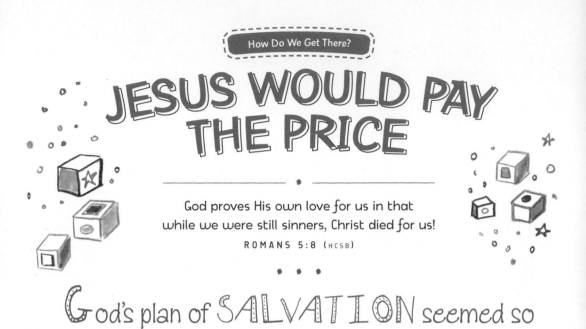

JESUS WOULD PAY THE PRICE

God proves His own love for us in that
while we were still sinners, Christ died for us!

ROMANS 5:8 (HCSB)

God's plan of SALVATION seemed so

unfair.

Why would His perfect Son pay the

cost?

To show us His love and save us from

sin,

Precious Jesus would die on a

CROSS!

JESUS GAVE HIS PERFECT LIFE FOR YOU AND ME

Christ never sinned! But God treated him as a sinner,
so that CHRIST could make us acceptable to God.

2 CORINTHIANS 5:21 (CEV)

• • •

By faith, we believe in the

Bible,

And it tells of a great

MYSTERY:

How do boys and girls get to

heaven?

They trust Jesus and simply

believe.

GOD MADE JESUS ALIVE AGAIN

They killed him by nailing him to a cross. But on the third day
God raised him from the dead.

ACTS 10:39-40 (NIrV)

• • •

But that's not the end of the

story.

Lord Jesus has risen—it's

true!

Now Jesus is living in

heaven,

And we'll live FOREVER there

too!

JESUS IS OUR ONLY WAY TO HEAVEN

Jesus answered, "I am the way and the truth and the life.
No one comes to the Father except through me."

JOHN 14:6 (NIV)

• • •

So where will the saints live **forever?**

In heaven with Jesus, you **know!**

But there's only one way to get **there.**

TRUST Jesus, for He loves you **so!**

76

BIG QUESTIONS

Yes, we are of good courage, and we would rather be
away from the body and at home with the Lord.

2 CORINTHIANS 5:8 (ESV)

• • •

I must ask you two very big **questions.**

The answers are easy, I **know.**

Do you want to see Jesus in **heaven?**

Is heaven where you want to **go?**

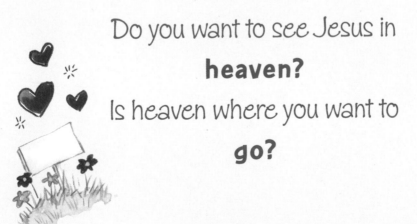

78

HEAVEN'S PRAYER

If you confess with your mouth that Jesus is Lord and believe in your heart that God raised him from the dead, you will be saved.

ROMANS 10:9 (ESV)

• • •

So if you want to love **Jesus,**

Then say this little prayer with **me.**

Lord, I know You died on the **cross**

And gave Your life to set me **free!**

AMAZING GRACE HOW SWEET THE SOUND

ANOTHER HOUSE IN HEAVEN

When everything is ready, I will come and get you, so that you will always be with me where I am.

JOHN 14:3

• • •

If you have asked Jesus into your

HEART,

He's building a house just for

you.

And soon—very soon—He's coming

again,

So heaven can be your home

too!

HOME
SWEET
HOME

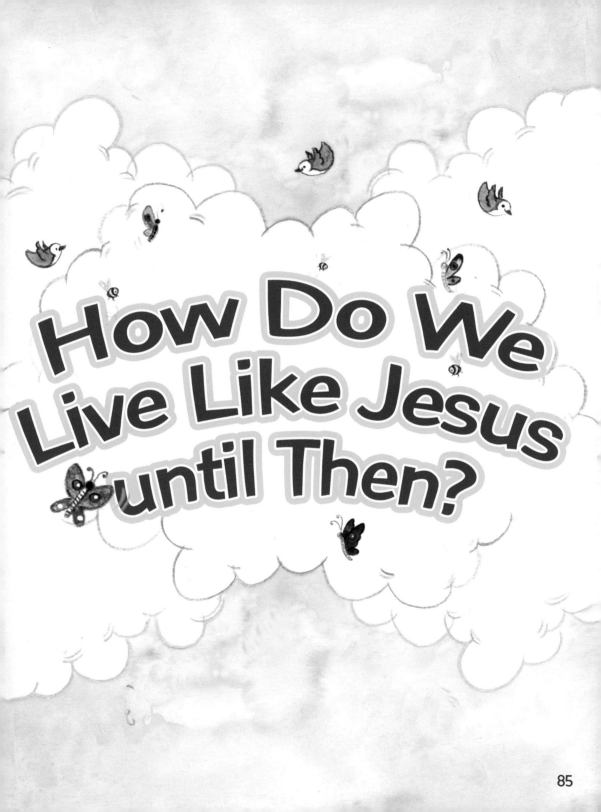

How Do We Live Like Jesus until Then?

WE LIVE LIKE JESUS

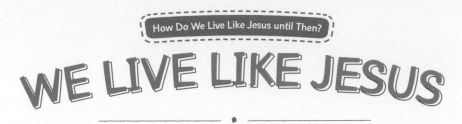

Follow God's example . . . and walk in the way of love,
just as Christ loved us and gave himself up for us.

EPHESIANS 5:1-2 (NIV)

• • •

Until we stand at heaven's

GATE

And with angels enter

in,

Let's live like Jesus said to

live:

Love others and walk with

Him.

How can we live like Jesus?

(Answer: Follow His example)

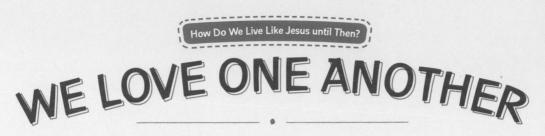

WE LOVE ONE ANOTHER

Love the LORD your God with all your heart, all your soul,
and all your mind. . . . Love your neighbor as yourself.

MATTHEW 22:37-39

• • •

Jesus began each

morning

The way my day should

start.

He loved others as

Himself

And God with all His

heart!

How can we live like Jesus?

(Answer: Love others)

WE SERVE ONE ANOTHER

Even the Son of Man came not to be served but to serve others.

MARK 10:45

Jesus had come from

heaven

To SERVE and not to be

served.

Like Him, we serve

each other,

Gladly obeying

GOD'S WORD!

How can we live like Jesus?

(Answer: Serve others)

WE ARE PATIENT WITH ONE ANOTHER

Be patient with everyone.

1 THESSALONIANS 5:14

• • •

Jesus showed people great PATIENCE.

As they watched, great lessons they **learned.**

So let us be patient with **others.**

Maybe they'll do the same in **return!**

92

How can we live like Jesus?

(Answer: Be patient with others)

WE CARE FOR ONE ANOTHER

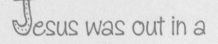

This makes for harmony . . . so that all the [people] care for each other.

1 CORINTHIANS 12:25

• • •

Jesus was out in a

sailboat.

A storm came, but He calmed the

sea.

He cared for His friends, who were

FRIGHTENED!

And that's the friend I want to

be!

How can we live like Jesus?

(Answer: Care for others)

WE ARE KIND TO ONE ANOTHER

Be kind to each other.
EPHESIANS 4:32

Jesus was kind to children He **met.**

He spoke in soft, loving **tones.**

So may our words be gentle and **kind,**

And make others feel right at **home!**

How can we live like Jesus?

(Answer: Be kind to others)

WE HELP ONE ANOTHER

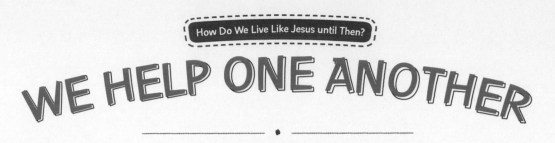

God has appointed in the CHURCH... helpers.

1 CORINTHIANS 12:28 (RSV)

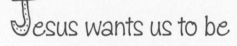

Jesus wants us to be

helpers,

Who take time to help those in

need.

I want to love and serve

others.

'Cause the Lord wants good helpers

indeed!

How can we live like Jesus?

(Answer: Help others)

WE FELLOWSHIP AND PLAY WITH ONE ANOTHER

If we walk in the light, as he is in the light,
we have fellowship one with another.

1 JOHN 1:7 (KJV)

• • •

Jesus said He is the light of the

world,

And those who love Jesus shine

too.

Whenever God's children gather and

play,

The Light of the World can shine

through!

How can we live like Jesus?

(Answer: Fellowship and play with one another)

WE SPEAK THE TRUTH TO ONE ANOTHER

Tell the truth to each other.

ZECHARIAH 8:16

Sometimes the TRUTH is easy to **tell.**

Sometimes it's harder to **do.**

But let all our words be like **Jesus:**

Loving and HONEST and **true!**

How can we live like Jesus?

(Answer: Tell the truth)

WE SHOW KINDNESS AND MERCY TO ONE ANOTHER

Show mercy and kindness to one another.

ZECHARIAH 7:9

If someone is hurting or **lonely,**

What is it God wants us to **do?**

Show them some kindness and MERCY.

Treat them like that someone is **you!**

How can we live like Jesus?

(Answer: Show kindness and mercy)

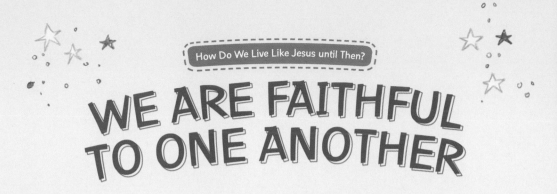

WE ARE FAITHFUL TO ONE ANOTHER

You are faithful to your promises, O my God.

PSALM 71:22

• • •

When GOD makes a promise, He **keeps it!**

He's FAITHFUL in all of His **ways.**

And we should be faithful like **Jesus**

So others can trust what we **say!**

How can we live like Jesus?

(Answer: Be faithful to keep our promises)

WE SHOW HOSPITALITY TO ONE ANOTHER

Don't forget to show hospitality to strangers, for some
who have done this have entertained angels without realizing it!

HEBREWS 13:2

Jesus always made people feel
WELCOME
With a word, with a smile, with a
touch.

When we show someone
HOSPITALITY,
It says that we love them
so much!

How can we live like Jesus?

(Answer: Show hospitality to others)

WE ARE COURTEOUS TO ONE ANOTHER

Finally, all of you be of one mind . . . be courteous.

1 PETER 3:8 (NKJV)

• • •

You won't hear a "No!" without

"Thank you."

You won't hear a "Yes!" without

"Please."

Be COURTEOUS. Practice good

manners.

God's happy with nice words like

these!

How can we live like Jesus?

(Answer: Be courteous to others)

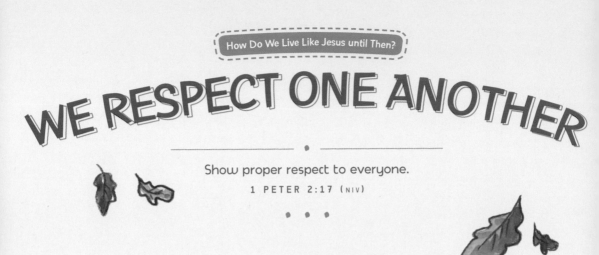

WE RESPECT ONE ANOTHER

Show proper respect to everyone.

1 PETER 2:17 (NIV)

• • •

Every boy and girl is so
SPECIAL,
Made by GOD and loved by Him
too!

So let us RESPECT all God has
made,
And He will be so proud of
you!

112

How can we live like Jesus?

(Answer: Show respect to everyone)

WE PRAY FOR ONE ANOTHER

Always be joyful. Never stop praying.
1 THESSALONIANS 5:16-17 (NIrV)

Jesus prayed for His dear
friends
When they were sick or
scared.

God hears every word we
say
When we call out in
PRAYER!

114

How can we live like Jesus?

(Answer: Pray for others every day)

WE COMFORT ONE ANOTHER

Comfort one another with these words.

1 THESSALONIANS 4:18 (KJV)

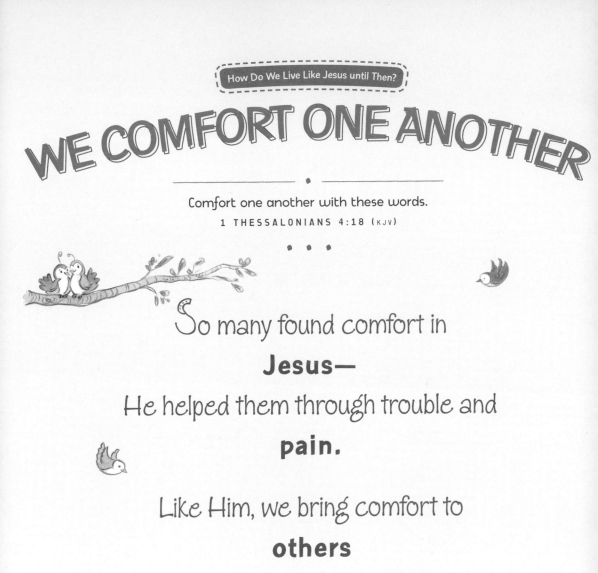

So many found comfort in

Jesus—

He helped them through trouble and

pain.

Like Him, we bring comfort to

others

Whenever we share Jesus'

name.

How can we live like Jesus?

(Answer: Comfort others)

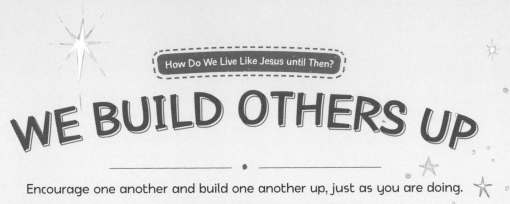

WE BUILD OTHERS UP

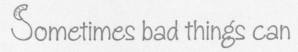

Encourage one another and build one another up, just as you are doing.

1 THESSALONIANS 5:11 (ESV)

• • •

Sometimes bad things can

happen—

Something said, something done, something

heard.

When this happens to someone you

know,

Build them up with ENCOURAGING

words.

How can we live like Jesus?

(Answer: Build others up)

WE ARE PEACEMAKERS

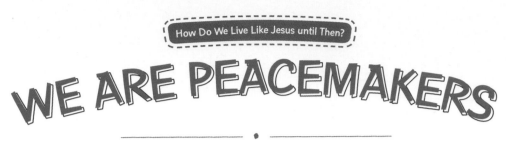

Blessed are the peacemakers: for they shall be called the children of God.

MATTHEW 5:9 (KJV)

Two kids are fighting. They want the same **toy.**

That isn't what Jesus would **do!**

He'd be a PEACEMAKER, happy to **share.**

So let's all be peacemakers **too!**

120

How can we live like Jesus?

(Answer: Be peacemakers)

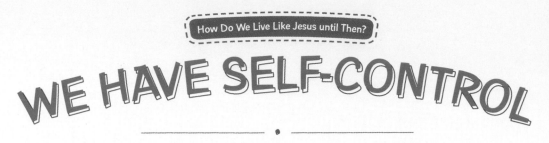

WE HAVE SELF-CONTROL

The fruit of the Spirit is love, joy, peace, . . . and self-control.

GALATIANS 5:22–23 (NIV)

I shouldn't say all that I **want.**

I shouldn't do all that I **feel.**

For God has given me SELF-CONTROL,

So now I can do His good **will.**

How can we live like Jesus?

(Answer: Show self-control)

WE ARE JOYFUL

The joy of the LORD is your strength.
NEHEMIAH 8:10 (NIV)

• • •

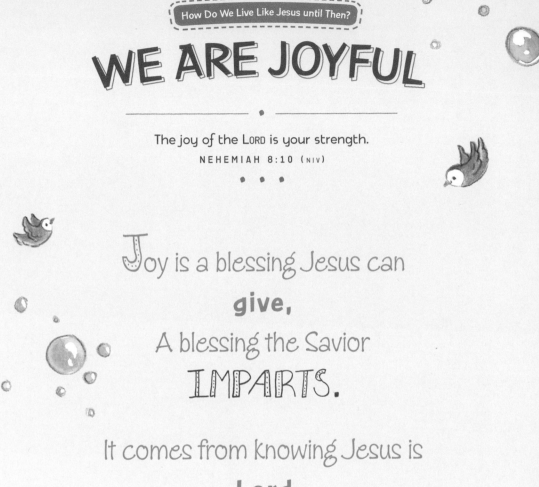

Joy is a blessing Jesus can

give,

A blessing the Savior

IMPARTS.

It comes from knowing Jesus is

Lord

And living inside of your

heart!

How can we live like Jesus?

(Answer: Be joyful)

GLOSSARY OF BIBLE WORDS

ANGELS	Heavenly beings who serve God and bring people messages from Him
ASTOUND	To amaze
BIBLE	The book that tells God's message to boys and girls
CHRIST	Means "Messiah," the One sent by God to save us from sin
CHURCH	A gathering of the people who believe in Jesus
COURTEOUS	Being nice and helping another person in a kind way
CRAFTED	Made with knowledge and skill
CREATION	Everything in the whole universe, which God made out of nothing
CROSS	The wooden posts on which Jesus died
DELIGHT	Happiness
DISOBEY	To do something you were told not to do
ENCOURAGING	Cheering, uplifting, kind
ETERNAL	Never-ending; always one more day
FAITH	Believing in what you cannot see and acting upon it
FAITHFUL	Always doing what you say you will do; being someone people can trust
FATHER (GOD)	Another name for Yahweh (God)
FOREVER	For a very, very long time
FRIGHTENED	Scared or afraid
GATE	The place where you enter in; the doorway
GLORY	Honor and respect
GOD	The Creator and Ruler of all things
GOD'S WORD	The Bible; God's instruction book
HEART	Where a person's deepest feelings are
HEAVEN	The eternal place where God lives and rules; where people who love and follow Jesus go when they die
HEROES	Men and women who do great things; people we want to be like
HONEST	Telling the truth; doing what is right
HOSPITALITY	Making people feel at home; being friendly and kind to others when they visit us
IDEA	A thought or plan about what to do
IMPARTS	Makes known; gives to others
JESUS	The Son of God; the Messiah sent from God to save us from sin
KINGDOM	A place where a king is the ruler

LAMB OF GOD	A name for Jesus that means He is perfect and holy
LANGUAGE	The words people use when they talk; our language is English
MERCY	Being kind and caring to someone who is sad or has done something wrong
MYSTERY	Something we do not understand
NATION	A country; a big group of people who live in the same place
PATIENCE	Staying quiet and calm when we have to wait
PEACEMAKER	Someone who shares, tries to get along with others, and does not start fights
PEAK	The very top of a high mountain
PEARLS	Gems that form inside the shell of an oyster (a sea animal)
PRAISE	Saying "thank you" and "I love you" to God
PRAYER	Talking to God
PRECIOUS	Something rare and valuable
PROCLAIM	To tell
PROMISE	To give your word that you will do something
RESPECT	To treat people nicely and think of them as worthy and important
REWARD	A prize or payment for doing a good job
SAINTS	People who are going to heaven
SALVATION	Being saved from sin and death when we believe in Jesus
SAVIOR	The One who saves or rescues us; Jesus
SELF-CONTROL	Not doing everything you feel; stopping yourself from doing something bad
SEPARATED	Set apart; moved away from something
SERVE	To work for others and do things that will help them
SIN	Disobeying the law of God
SPECIAL	One of a kind; excellent
TRIBE	A group of related people
TRUST	To believe; to be sure of someone or something
TRUTH	What is real and true; the opposite of a lie
WELCOME	A friendly greeting; making someone feel at home
WISDOM	Understanding; using knowledge to make the right choice
YAHWEH	The name of God